FLORIDA'S ASHLEY GANG

by

Ada Coats Williams

Copyright 1996, and all other rights are reserved by the author, Ada Coats Williams, and her heirs.
ISBN 0-912451-28-9
Reprinted by agreement with the author
Florida Classics Library
P. O. Box 1657
Port Salerno, FL 34992

Prepared in Fort Pierce, Florida, April 1983, for presentation at the May 1983 meeting of the Florida State Historical Society.

DEDICATED

To the memory of DeSoto Tiger and his wife, Ada Micco;

To their children: Willie and Flora Tiger, and Flora's husband, Willie Jones;

To their grandchildren: Addie Osceola, Bert Jones, and Louise Jones Gopher;

To their great-grandchildren: Rodney, Reno, Abigail, Ramsey, and Bill Osceola; Patrick Jones, Rita and Carla Gopher; and Stacey and Duane Jones.

FLORIDA'S ASHLEY GANG

This great state of Florida
Has had men both noble and brave,
But it's also had its wicked ones,
Who've sent many to an early grave.

This is the first verse of a ballad about Florida's Ashley Gang.

John Ashley, the purported leader of this infamous gang, in December of 1911, robbed a group of Seminole Indians of their furs, killing one of them, DeSoto Tiger. Tiger was a son of one of the most highly respected Seminole chiefs, Chief Tom Tiger.

DeSoto Tiger, as was his father, was known to be a man of integrity and was respected by the white pioneers.

With the commission of this crime, John Ashley became a hunted criminal, and for the next thirteen years, he lead his gang in bootlegging, rum-running, train and bank robberies, jail and prison escapes, and murdering.

On November 1, 1924, John Ashley and some of his gang were captured and killed on the Sebastian Bridge.

From 1924 until 1983, a great debate raged as to what really happened on the bridge that night. Was the gang shot when they tried to escape, as the deputies involved testified under oath, or were they handcuffed and executed by St. Lucie County Sheriff Merritt and his deputies? In 1983 the truth was finally learned about what happened that night, November 1, 1924, on the Sebastian Bridge.

One first needs to know, however, what life on the southern part of Florida was like at the beginning of the twentieth century when these events occurred.

Though the lower east coast of the peninsula of Florida was the first location to be marked with a name (Canaveral) on the early maps of the New World, this area was one of the last frontiers to be settled. Attempts at settlement had been made by the mightiest governments of that time — Spain, England, France, and the United

States — but each had failed. Even though the United States Government removed almost the entire nation of Seminoles from the area to encourage settlement, authorizing and outfitting the Indian River Colony in 1842 for the purpose of colonization, it also failed.

This part of the peninsula, so richly endowed by the Creator, remained a tropical wilderness, warmed and cooled by the winds that blew up from the waters — waters filled with the shining bodies of fish that swam and played, jumping out of her depths for brief moments with the sun and the sky. The land abounded with creatures of the wild: turkey, quail, deer, and bear. The land and the water remained a tropical Eden, sustaining the small band of Seminoles who had escaped capture and banishment, as they slowly worked their way back from the Everglades where they had sought refuge.

But now the time had come on God's calendar of the universe for this tropical jungle to abandon her wild freedom and at last to give birth to a new bit of America, here along the waters of the Indian River.

In the late 1860's and early 1870's, individual families began coming in and homesteading at points far apart along the river. Soon others began to follow, and small settlements grew that became known as Cocoa, Eau Gallie, Vero, Fort Pierce, Stuart, Gomez, Salerno, Palm Beach, and Miami. Many of these settlements were far from the county seats that governed them: Fort Pierce was a southernmost settlement in Brevard County, with the county seat eighty miles up the coast at Titusville, and Stuart's county seat was West Palm Beach. In each instance, the county officials were many miles away and had little concern for the small settlements. These people had to rely upon themselves for survival and governance. Their only highway was the river; there were no doctors, stores, hospitals, or pharmacies. They had to rely upon their personal stamina, home remedies and whiskey, their love for the land, and their belief in God for their safety and endurance. They came from every part of the United States and for many different reasons. Some were families of the Confederacy: families who had lost their homes, their land, and their way of life. They were seeking new lands and a new beginning. Some came for reasons of health: persons who had the dreaded disease, consumption; or, perhaps some other type of respiratory ailment; or the "withering disease," cancer. There were no miracle drugs then, and the afflicted ones were advised to seek a mild climate. Others were just adventurous souls who sought the new and daring; some were fleeing from the "law" and sought a place remote from city and county governments. They were all rugged individualists: persons who had the courage of their convictions and the daring to cast their lot with others in opening and developing a new territory.

Henry Flagler, another with faith in this river country,

invested, at great personal financial risk, in the building of a railway that opened up the coast and hastened further development.

Now there was a quicker way to come and go, one that was not dependent upon the caprice of the weather. Now supplies for stores could be brought in on a regular basis; now others had an incentive to join with the early settlers. Doctors, pharmacists, and teachers came. The fishermen and farmers had a way to ship their harvests from river and farms. The building of the railway provided work for laborers, and the maintenance and running of the railway provided steady employment for permanent residents.

With the coming of the twentieth century, the lower east coast had organized governments in the little settlements: cities became incorporated and elected city officials. Their county governments were still a great distance from them, however, and often rough, undisciplined characters followed the railroad construction. By the time a law official could be notified and dispatched the distance to make an arrest, the offender would be gone. Local lads were soon taking the law into their own hands. They formed their own law enforcement agency known as the Board of the Barrel of Correction. They would catch the rowdy ones, take them down into town, bend them over a barrel, and give them a sound thrashing. They were known to take harsher measures with the worst offenders: taking them on horseback into the woods, making them drop their trousers, horsewhipping them until they drew blood, and leaving them to ride back into town on hard saddles.

In 1904, Joseph Ashley moved his wife and nine children into the area. He had come from Fort Myers, near the Caloosahatchee River, and settled near Pompano, Florida, seeking employment with the railroad as a wood chopper.[1] This was steady employment, for the huge "steel horses" burned wood to produce the steam to power the engines. His move may have been prompted by a feud that resulted in a "bit of gunplay" in which the one whom he wounded chose not to identify his assailant, but declared that he would settle the score in his own way.[2]

The older sons in the family worked as wood choppers, and the younger ones hunted and fished. The family made friends with the settlers, and in 1906, one son, Bill, married a local Pompano girl.[3]

In 1911, Joe Ashley had moved his family farther north up the coast to West Palm Beach. There he still chopped wood for the Florida East Coast Railway, farmed, and fished. Just when the family started operating a still and dealing in bootlegging is not known, but it soon became common knowledge among their acquaintances. John Ashley was now spending a great deal of time camping in the woods and trapping. There was a good market for otter hides, and his brother Bill often camped and trapped with the Seminoles. Some of the Indians liked to have the boys join them, for the Ashleys usually brought liquor into their camps. They especially liked Bill Ashley; he had convinced them that he was their friend. It was because of this association with Bill that they welcomed John Ashley when he asked to camp and trap with them in December 1911.[4]

News accounts of the events that followed state that John Ashley and a Seminole, DeSoto Tiger, trapping partners, left their camp to take their hides to market. John Ashley arrived in Miami alone and sold the hides for $1200 to Girtman Brothers. On December 29, 1911, the body of DeSoto Tiger was dredged up by a dredging crew. The Indian had been shot, and John Ashley was charged with his murder.[5]

Frank Shore, an elderly Seminole Medicine Man, living on the Brighten Reservation at Brighton, Florida, a brother-in-law of DeSoto Tiger, discredits much of the news accounts. Frank Shore has stated that a group of Indians had been trapping for otter hides, which brought ten dollars a hide — a lot of money in those days. John Ashley appeared at camp one day and asked if he could camp and hunt with them for awhile. Since he was a brother of their friend Bill, they welcomed him. At the time the Indians had eighty or more hides, and they decided to quit a few days to go home for Christmas.

DeSoto Tiger had seen his newborn baby daughter, Flora, only once before he had had to leave for the hunt, and he was anxious to return to his wife, Ada Micco, and their babe. It was their custom to take the hides to the operator of a dredging outfit that was dredging the canal from Lake Okeechobee that would lead to the Atlantic Ocean at Fort Lauderdale. The operator, Captain Fowry, was a good friend of the Indians and they trusted him. As they collected large numbers of hides, they often would take them to him to keep while they went out to trap for more. They decided that DeSoto Tiger would take the hides to Fowry, and that they would break up camp until after Christmas. As Tiger poled away from the shore, Ashley called out to ask if he could go with him. He said that he needed to buy a few supplies from Captain Fowry. Tiger poled back to the shore. Ashley picked up his Winchester gun and gear, and climbed into Tiger's dugout canoe. That was the last that the Indians saw of Tiger until his body was brought up from the canal December 29, 1911. Frank Shore said that they never reached Captain Fowry. Fowry saw a canoe pass far in the distance, off among the marsh grasses. He saw that a lone rider was in the canoe, but it was too far away for him to notice who he was. Tiger and Ashley had left early in the morning, and when they had not returned by noon, the Indians began to wonder what had happened to them.[6]

On the evening of December 28, 1911, John was arrested in West Palm Beach for the reckless display of firearms. He paid a twenty-five-dollar fine and departed. After the Indian's body was discovered on December 29, Sheriff George Baker, of Palm Beach County, sent deputies to find John Ashley.[7]

The late Hix C. Stuart, a resident of the area in which the Ashley's lived and operated, recorded in his book *The Notorious Ashley Gang* that Deputy Sheriffs Barfield and Hannon were dispatched to a location in Hobe Sound where John Ashley was believed to be hiding. As they walked along the old Dixie Highway, John and his brother, Bob, stepped out of the palmettos, held up the deputies, and disarmed them. The Ashleys taunted them with these words: "Tell Baker not to send any more chicken-hearted men with rifles, or they are apt to get hurt." With this humiliation, they sent the deputies on their way, later sending their guns back to Sheriff Baker by a friend. John left the state, going to New Orleans where he worked on a boat for a time, and then to Seattle, Washington, where he worked in a logging camp.

The Ashleys were a loyal and closely knit family, and soon John grew lonesome for them. He returned to Florida in 1914 and sent word that he was ready to surrender. He had no fear of being tried for the murder of DeSoto Tiger. He readily admitted killing him, but said that he did so in self-defense. He figured that no jury of Florida crackers would convict him for killing an Indian, especially since he was the only living witness to the incident. John's attorney, M. D. Carmichael of West Palm Beach, arranged for John to surrender near the family home in Gomez. He asked not to be handcuffed, and the request was honored. He was reported to be a model prisoner, giving Deputy Robert C. Baker, the county jailor, no trouble.[8]

The first trial of John Ashley for the murder of DeSoto Tiger was July 3, 1914, and ended in a mistrial. A copy of John's testimony was printed in the fiftieth anniversary edition of *The Stuart Times*, January 9, 1964. He gave his age as 27, and testified that DeSoto Tiger threatened to shoot him if he didn't give him some liquor. He had judged the reaction of the local citizens correctly, for the jury voted nine for acquittal and three for conviction.[9]

After the mistrial, the second trial was held, and the prosecution asked for a change of venue to Dade County. The Ashleys were greatly alarmed about this. When court adjourned, it was starting to rain and the sky was growing dark. John, still unhandcuffed, was escorted to the jail by young Deputy Sheriff Bob Baker, the jailor. The jail yard was fenced in with chicken wire. Baker went to unlock the jail door, and Mrs. Baker brought out a plate of food that Ashley's mother had left for him. Ashley held the plate while Baker turned on the light and started to unlock the door. Quickly, Ashley threw down the plate, bolted over the fence, and disappeared into the darkness. Baker jumped on a bicycle and went in hot pursuit. The prisoner had escaped.

The authorities believed that Ashley was hiding in the Everglades. During this time, he evidently joined with three criminals who had come down from Chicago: Clarence Middleton, a dope addict; Kid Lowe, a bank robber; and Roy Matthews.[10]

The February 12, 1915 issue of *The Stuart Times* carried a story of a "Daring Train Robbery," and once again John Ashley made the front page of his hometown newspaper. He was not a success as a train robber. One of the ladies whom he was attempting to rob escaped and ran screaming through the train. A quick-thinking porter locked the door between the cars, and the robbers could not enter. The train stopped a mile south of Stuart, and the would-be robbers fled.[11]

The law officials failed to locate John and his accomplices. In desperation, they arrested John's nephew, Hanford Mobley. The local paper was critical of the arrest. The story was carried on the front page, February 19, 1915, and it carefully mentioned all of the jobs Mobley held and ended with, "As far as can be learned, his record is clear and what prompted Sheriff Baker to arrest the man on such a charge, is hard to realize." John's father, Joe Ashley, and a colored man who worked for him, had also been arrested. All three were released quickly. Once again the law officials had suffered public embarrassment from the Ashleys.[12]

A week later, however, the local paper had headlines that read, "A Very Bold Robbery." John, his brother Bob, and Kid Lowe — now referred to by the paper as the Ashley Gang — had robbed the Bank of Stuart of $4,500.00.[13]

The bank robbery was more successful than the attempted train heist, but it was far from a professional job. John Ashley exhibited an ignorance of banks. He was also very trusting of those he was robbing, and thus easily fooled. He insisted that the bank officials open the desk drawers to check for money, but failed to notice the cash drawer that held a large sum of money. He demanded that they open the safety deposit boxes, only to learn from Mr. John Taylor that the owners had both keys. He apologized, saying: "I'll tell you, boy, it is a case where we need the money, and we just have got to have it. We were disappointed two weeks ago."[14] It is assumed that he referred to the aborted holdup of the Palm Beach Limited. The bandits then ordered the men in the bank (Cashier Wallace, the Messrs. Frank Coventry, Theo Tyndall, John E. Taylor, and K. H. Bentel) to hold their hands over their heads and leave the bank. They ordered Frank Coventry to get into his car to drive them. The robbers started firing their pistols to show that they meant business. Kid Lowe, angry because of the small "take," purposely shot John Ashley. The bullet shattered his jaw and came to rest against an eye, causing the loss of vision and the subsequent removal of the eye. When they had reached a planned destination, they ordered Coventry to hurry back to town. They fled in an automobile that was hidden in the woods.[15]

The alarm went out all over the state. Now they were wanted by the Federal Indian Agents, the Florida East Coast Railway, and the banking company.

Posses were formed, but they had trouble finding enough automobiles. When the owners learned for whom they were searching, they suddenly decided that the cars were not mechanically sound.

Naha and Tom Tiger, brothers of the slain DeSoto Tiger, were active in the search, and they helped to lead the posses to the camp after Sheriff Baker learned of the location from secretly hearing Bill Ashley call a doctor to go to attend to John's wound. Bill was in the camp with John when the camp was surrounded. He was not arrested, however, for all of the robbers were unmasked and easily recognized. Bob Ashley and Kid Lowe had left the camp the previous night and had escaped; but John, gravely wounded, had had to stay. His brother, Bill, in true Ashley family tradition, had gone to take care of him.[16]

The hometown paper had shown tolerance and

sympathy for the Ashleys in their earlier troubles; for example, "It seems ... every time a gun is discharged..., the crime is fastened on John Ashley... Also he cannot be accused of the murder of the Indian until it is so proven."[17]

Now, however, the tone became critical, perhaps even outraged, as the hometown "Bad-Boys" started perpetrating illegal acts upon the hometown.

The news account of the capture reviewed John's past incarceration and escape, adding his two recent robberies to the charge of murder, concluding: "It is hoped that neither Sheriff Baker nor his deputies will take any chances this time, and that Ashley gets what he deserves."[18]

A personal feud was growing between the law enforcement men and John Ashley. His ability to elude capture, his popularity with the native crackers in the area, and his taunting of the legal officers when he outsmarted them, caused the name Ashley to evoke bitterness and a desire to "get him."

The Ashley sons (Bill, Ed, Frank, Bob, and John), like all pioneer youths, learned to shoot well at an early age, and they had the best of teachers. Joe Ashley, their father, had a reputation for being a champion marksman. He was soon equaled by his son John, and this skill now made John the envy and the fear of the law enforcement officers. His reputation with the gun spread rapidly as men recalled hunting trips they had taken with him, or target practice they had witnessed. It was a favorite topic in the saloons and barbershops. One of the best displays of his skill was his ability to shoot through the mouth of a bottle, placed on its side on the top of a fence post, and blow out the bottom of the bottle without cracking the small mouth through which the bullet passed. Some recalled seeing him shoot the head off a quail with his revolver, from a distance of thirty or forty feet, as he rode through the woods in his wagon.[19] These stories caused the men in the posses to have a great respect for his fast draw and accurate aim, and when they closed in on him at various times, their caution proved to his advantage, as they took cover, enabling him to escape.

The small coastal communities now had an exciting topic of conversation — the exploits of the Ashley Gang. Now, along with the usual topics on the front page of the local newspapers (meetings of the Mozart Club, the P.T.A., church activities, and eulogies for local citizens who had "gone to their reward") appeared the latest news of John Ashley and his cohorts, several of whom were his brothers and his nephew, Hanford Mobley. There was a mixture of feelings of fear and defensiveness among the inhabitants: fear among the businessmen and bankers who might be targets for a robbery, and a feeling of defensiveness among neighbors and acquaintances who had known the Ashley family's friendship and hospitality. This large family often helped persons in trouble, and extended warm hospitality to any who came to their humble home. The children were known to be courteous to their elders, and excelled in those activities that pioneer men admired and deemed desirable qualities in a "real man." Young Hanford Mobley, John's nephew who became an active member of the Gang while still a teenager, was a popular boy at school. He was well liked by his teachers and his classmates. He was known to be polite, pleasant, and fun to be with. He often drove the family Model T Ford to school, and the highlight of the school day was to be asked to be one of the ten or so who would pile into the car at the lunch hour and cruise down the main street of Stuart. He was remembered by one of his classmates as being an average student and a good athlete, nice looking, and popular. His participation in the robberies was blamed on the influence of his Uncle John, whom Hanford idolized.[20]

John's need for medical care of the wound received at the time of the robbery of the Stuart Bank was the cause of his capture. He was in great pain and he surrendered without resistance. He was taken to the jail in Palm Beach, arriving at 5:30 p.m. on Thursday, March 4, 1915, where he was held to be tried for the murder of DeSoto Tiger.

There he received treatment for his wound, refusing to let the doctor operate to remove the bullet that was lodged in his head, his reason being that there was not much point in their going to that trouble if they planned to hang him for DeSoto Tiger's murder. John's eye had to be removed, and a glass eye was made for him. Word spread rapidly about the loss of his eye. There was speculation about how the loss would affect his shooting skill. They were to learn, in days to come, however, that he always must have shot with one eye shut, or that his skill was so superior to most, that even with this loss, he was still the expert marksman.

The March 26, 1915, edition of *The Stuart Times* reported that John Ashley would be tried in Dade County. Judge Branning ordered the change of venue after the court had exhausted a venire of 150 men who had been summoned "to serve their country." (Women, who did not have the right to vote in Florida in 1915, were not called "to serve their country" on jury duty.) The news account continued: "When the case had been called for trial, Ashley stated that he had not procured legal service and Judge Branning appointed Jerome E. Wideman and Col. F. Pope to defend him. Judge Branning then spoke to the veniremen and stated that those who were sick, or deaf, or had urgent business would be excused. In an instant there was a rush to the front of the courtroom, and about every ailment known to doctors was given out. In fact, Judge Branning was surprised to hear of so much sickness. About seventy-five were excused, and after a long drill by lawyers on both sides, but two jurors were secured."[21]

John Ashley was transferred to the jail in Miami to await trial for the murder of DeSoto Tiger. Clifford J. Clements served as interpreter for the Seminoles at the trial. Clements, a linguists who spoke twelve languages, had come from Petersburg, Virginia to Okeechobee, Florida on a hunting trip.

He met and married Miss Adaline Raulerson, daughter of the Peter and Louisiana Raulerson family, the first white family to move into the Okeechobee area.

Clements remained in Okeechobee after his marriage and studied the Seminole language. Thus he was well qualified to assist the Seminoles who had accepted the Raulerson family as trusted friends.

The Stuart Times, on April 2, 1915, carried a short notice of John Ashley's trial, recording that the jury was secured and that Assistant State Attorney Worley of Miami opened the case for the state with a brief statement, and then called the first witness, Captain Fowry, to the stand. The dredge operator told of finding the body of Tiger in the canal with a bullet hole through his head. The paper reported that the defendant appeared in good spirits and was being represented by Attorneys Bowen and Rose of Miami.[22]

The trial was a short one, and on April 6, 1915, John Ashley was found guilty as charged, and was sentenced to death by hanging.

The April 16, 1915, edition of *The Stuart Times* carried a short item of a refusal of a new trial for John Ashley in Miami. It stated that the court would pay for appeal to the Supreme Court and that the lawyers would do the work without pay. Ashley was reported as not having much hope about the outcome and was willing to submit to his fate. He still insisted that he was justified in killing DeSoto Tiger.[23]

While John Ashley awaited the appeal, he received home cooked meals from his mother, who worried over his condition and care. He also received a tonic that she had "Dr. Anner" (Dr. Anna Darrow of Okeechobee) prescribe for him. His sisters observed a jailor throwing out a meal of fried chicken that they had taken to him, and so his family became greatly concerned about his welfare. His brother, Bob, decided to relieve their anxiety by rescuing John from his confinement.[24]

Bob Ashley journeyed to Miami on June 2, 1915, and that afternoon he went to the home of the jailer, Deputy Sheriff Wilber Hendrickson, and knocked on his door. When Hendrickson opened the door, Bob Ashley asked if he were Hendrickson, and without giving him time to reply, killed him and took the keys to the jail. Mrs. Hendrickson rushed into the room at the sound of the shot, grabbed a gun, and unsuccessfully attempted to stop Bob. The gunshots were heard by others who rushed to the scene. Bob Ashley became frightened, dropped the keys, and ran across the street to a garage.

He dodged from street to street, finally stopping a car driven by T. F. Durkett, and demanded that Durkett take him out to a country road. Durkett refused; he stopped the car and told Ashley he could drive it himself.

Two policemen overtook Ashley at the corner of Eighth Street and Avenue I. One of them, Officer Bob Riblett, engaged Ashley in a gun fight. Riblett advanced toward Ashley and told him that he was under arrest. Ashley fired at him, wounding the officer mortally, but not before Riblett returned the fire. Both men were taken to the hospital, and both died a few hours later. A full account of the attempted jailbreak was recorded on the front page of the June 6, 1921, edition of *The Stuart Times*.[25]

It was believed that Bob Ashley acted alone. When John appeared grieved at his brother's condition, the sheriff of Dade County attempted to get him to his brother, but Bob died before the visit could be arranged. Ed Rogers, a brother-in-law of the Ashleys, went to Miami to claim the slain brother's body, and the sorrowing Ashleys buried him in the family cemetery close to their home. He was to be but the first of a number of the Ashley men who would be buried there, as they too would die violent deaths.

Rumors began to spread that there was an organized

movement to remove John from jail. Sheriff Hardie of Dade County placed extra guards with sawed off shotguns at the jail. They waited in vain. Rumor also speculated that John was paying for his defense with the money stolen from the Stuart Bank, even though Bob Ashley confessed that he and Kid Lowe had divided the money and had taken it for their escape at the time that John was captured.

On July 25, 1915, an article appeared in *The Stuart Times* with the information that the American Fidelity and Deposit Company of Baltimore, insurers for the Stuart Bank, had mailed a check for one hundred dollars to the widow of Officer Riblett for his part in apprehending and capturing one of the bank robbers. The article also stated that she would continue to receive the deceased husband's monthly check.[26]

In November 1915, John Ashley attempted to break out of jail. It was a peaceful attempt, with his only weapon, a spoon. For five weeks he had patiently dug away the dirt with an iron spoon, after he had broken a hole in the cement floor of his cell. He would store in his closet the dirt that he dug, and later he would flush it away with water. The jailor discovered the project one day while Ashley was taking his daily free hour in the corridors. The Sheriff decided not to let Ashley know that they had detected his plan. They wanted to observe to determine if others were involved in the planned escape. Ashley was only two feet away from liberty when they informed him that his plan had been discovered. He was furious, and blamed a condemned murderer, Floriah R. Crawford, for having reported him. The Sheriff denied the accusation.[27]

John Ashley remained in the jail in Dade County. Finally, August 11, 1916, word was received that the Supreme Court of Florida had reversed the decision of the circuit court and that the famous bandit would be given another chance for his life. His attorneys were successful in getting the charge of murder nol prosed, and Ashley was returned to Palm Beach County to stand trial for bank robbery. He pleaded guilty and was sentenced to seventeen and one-half years in the penitentiary at Raiford.

On November 23, 1916, John Ashley arrived at Raiford. He proved to be a model prisoner, and was sent to a road camp on March 31, 1918. He had been at the camp but a few months when he escaped with a notorious bank robber, Tom Maddox, and fled to the Everglades where his girlfriend, Laura Upthegrove awaited him.[28]

The July 11, 1918, edition of the *Stuart Messenger* (a name used for a period of time by *The Stuart Times*) had a front page account of the escape from the road camp at Milligan, Florida.[29]

Ashley remained at large almost three years after his

escape. He had many friends and family members in a five-county area who were glad to help hide him. Among these was Laura Upthegrove, a member of one of the old Florida families. She was the only woman who was ever linked romantically with John. She participated in all of the activities of the Gang: scouting for robberies, or directing the delivery of liquor. She was described by a reporter as a "large woman with dark hair, a deep suntan, and wore a .38 caliber revolver strapped to her waist." She was soon dubbed "Queen of the Everglades" because of her notorious activities in that area. She was believed to have a strong influence over the Gang members.

John Ashley apparently devoted his time during this period to operating three stills in Palm Beach County and joining with his two brothers, Ed and Frank, in running liquor to Florida from West End in the Bahama Islands, a lucrative business with the advent of the Prohibition Law in 1920. During this time it is reported that he used the name *Davis*. He was making a delivery of his contraband liquor to a garage near Wauchula when he was apprehended by Sheriff John Poucher. John had left his pistol in his car, so he surrendered peacefully. Sheriff Poucher was unaware of the true identify of his prisoner until a colored man in the Wauchula jail recognized Ashley and enlightened the sheriff. It was in June of 1921 that John Ashley was returned to the penitentiary at Raiford, Florida.[30]

While John was confined, his brothers, Ed and Frank, continued transporting liquor from the Islands. The British sold the best brands and there was a great demand for the liquor with prohibition closing down legal sources. Not only the Ashleys, but many persons of prominent families were now engaged in bootlegging. Men were making fortunes and the competition was ever increasing. These small frontier communities had few families who were not engaged either in transporting and selling the contraband liquor or in being a customer of those who were. Many families had never known what it was *not* to have liquor in the house for medicinal reasons, and to a large segment of the population, the federal law was just another example of the kind of regulation that they or their parents had tried to be relieved of when they decided to secede. Many law officials gladly took payoffs and simply looked in the opposite direction when the liquor was being transported. The Ashley family was known still to be strongly Confederate in their feelings. They used as their excuse for robbing the bank the fact that Yankees owned the insurance company and that it was one way to get the Yankee money back that was stolen from the South.

Rum-running became such big business that underworld characters came from the cities, and wars constantly broke out among them. Tragedy came to the Ashley family through this rum-running. Ed and Frank went over with $13,000 for a load, and were detained because of weather. When poor weather conditions persisted a second day, they started out for the mainland, in spite of warnings that the weather conditions were hazardous and that they were overloaded for the trip across. They never reached their destination, and it was at this same time that John Ashley, according to Hix Stuart, had a dream about three other rum-runners hijacking their boat and killing them. So real did the dream seem that he sent for his father.

The disappearance of Ed and Frank was never solved, and shortly thereafter the three rum-runners and hijackers also disappeared. There was great speculation as to whether they fell pray to weather, to other hijackers, or to Ashley vengeance.[31]

While John was at Raiford, different members of the Gang served as leader: sometimes it was Middleton, sometimes Matthews. Their activities mostly were the hijacking of other rum-runners' loads being transported by car or boat. Hanford Mobley had quit school and had become an active member of the Gang. He, Middleton, and Matthews planned once more to rob the Stuart Bank. Mobley, who was slight of build and youthful, dressed as a woman, wearing a white blouse, a long black skirt, and hat. He had a veil draped over his face for disguise. His accomplices were outside, looking in through the window. John Taylor was still an employee of the bank, and he once again found himself being robbed by the Ashley Gang.[32]

The robbers fled in a car that they had stolen from a resident in Gomez, after they had tied him to a tree. They were pursued by young Bob Baker who had followed his father as sheriff of Palm Beach County. With the cooperation of sheriffs across the state, the officials finally apprehended Mobley and Middleton in Plant City. They refused to identify the third robber. Middleton later made a full confession to Baker, begging not to be exposed to Mobley who would probably kill him. Baker then searched for Matthews who was caught in Griffin, Georgia.[33]

Hanford, as his Uncle John, had a penchant for breaking out of jail. After several attempts, he was moved to the Broward County jail that was believed to be a stronger facility. The new jailor, W. W. Hicks, gave the prisoners a great deal of freedom, and soon Mobley and Matthews were on their way out. Middleton refused to break out with them. He probably feared that they knew how Baker had learned of Matthews' identity. Middleton was sent to Raiford for fifteen years, and joined John Ashley, Ray Lynn, and Joe Tracey.[34]

Ray Lynn, one of the men killed on the bridge in 1924, was from an old Florida family.

He married young and joined the Army. Army life with its restrictions and discipline, proved unbearable for this country lad who had known such freedom to hunt and fish in frontier Florida. He went AWOL.

His young wife was pregnant, and she worried greatly about how they could live and raise a child under those circumstances.

Lynn, of course, had to go into hiding. His wife divorced him, and he hid out in the vast Florida Everglades where he soon joined up with John Ashley and his gang.

He joined in their boot-legging, rum-running, and robberies, but he was never known to have killed anyone.

John Ashley had again been sent to a road gang for good behavior, and once again he escaped. As he made his way out to the Everglades, he stopped in Okeechobee to get some supper at the house of one of his former customers. The man was cooking supper when he heard some pebbles hit his window. Upon stepping out on the porch, he found that John Ashley was crouching beside the steps. The man called out to ask what he wanted, and John answered that he was hungry. He was invited in to eat and was asked how he got out of Raiford. John grinned and said, "I broke out."

"How did you do that?" his host asked.

"I bribed a guard," responded Ashley. He finished eating and disappeared into the darkness of the night.

John Ashley was rumored to have killed a tramp.

According to the rumor, the man had caught a ride on a box car of a Florida East Coast train, as tramps often did those days. He went up to the back door of the Ashley home to ask for a handout of food. Mrs. Ashley was home alone, and she took pity on the man and served him a dish of food. As he ate, he observed that she was alone, and when he returned the plate, he grabbed her and raped her.

John, according to a close family member, hunted the man down and killed him. There was never a police or news account of this incident. At that time, the legal punishment for rape in Florida was the death sentence. The reason the family took the law into their hands was that they didn't want others to know, and thus save their mother the mortification of having her tragedy become public knowledge.

Shortly after John's escape, one of his gang members, Joe Tracey, completed his sentence at Raiford, and Ray Lynn and Clarence Middleton escaped from a road camp at Marianna, Florida. Hanford Mobley, who had escaped from the Broward County jail, had worked as a taxi driver in California, and had made several trips to Germany working on a trans-Atlantic liner. All returned to the Everglades and rejoined John.

The Gang engaged in many illegal enterprises: stealing cars, hijacking cars and boats loaded with liquor, robbing stores and banks. In between jobs and hiding out, they appeared in first one town and then another to shop, play pool, and get haircuts. Many people lived in terror of them; many others helped to protect them from the lawmen and considered them friends. Their range of operations expanded into the central part of the state. Their activities and their ability to break out of jails continued to keep the sheriffs of many counties frustrated and embarrassed.

On one occasion the men ordered diamond rings that were to be sent C.O.D. from the Duval Jewelry Store. When the Ashley Gang received notice of the arrival of the order, they broke into the Express office that night, taking only the diamond rings. Once again Yankee insurance companies could pay.[35]

St. Lucie County residents were also aware of the Ashley Gang's activities. On July 27, 1922, the *Stuart Messenger* carried an article about "Ex-Stuart People in the Limelight in Fort Pierce." The automobiles, belonging to Judge Parker, Ruhl Koblegard, and A. J. Lightfoot were stolen by members of the Gang, and later recovered by Saint Lucie County Sheriff J. R. Merritt. The outlaws frequently stole automobiles to haul their shine, and later abandoned them. This crime was committed so frequently that Sheriff Merritt's office reported recovering thirty automobiles in one month.[36]

The John Ashley-Bob Baker feud had developed into a bitter "to the death" rivalry. Ashley frequently sent

Sheriff Baker a bullet with a message that one just like it had his name on it. Sheriff Baker sent word back that one day he would wear John Ashley's glass eye as a watch fob. The populace was divided: many were outraged at the open lawlessness, while others enjoyed the friendship and generosity of the Gang.

In November 1923, John made plans to rob the Pompano bank. Pompano was a small but prosperous farming community. One of the Gang, Joe Tracey, went into town and hired a taxi. When they got out of town, he had the driver stop, and the other outlaws came out of the woods to join him. They ate a picnic lunch, practiced target shooting, then tied the driver to a tree and told him that they were going to rob the bank. They also told him where he could find his taxi after they finished with it. As they left, John gave him a rifle bullet, telling him to give it to Sheriff Baker and to tell the Sheriff that they would be waiting for him in the Everglades.

Their bank robbery was a success: they escaped with $5,000 in cash and $18,000 in securities. As John left the bank, he gave C. H. Cates, the cashier, a bullet, telling him that it was a souvenir of John's career as a bank robber. After the taxi driver had worked himself loose, he hurried into town to tell his story, and found his taxi right where they said it would be.[37]

Almost everyone had a story to tell about the Ashley Gang: they had left money under a brick on a poor, ill person's porch; they had left groceries at the door of a widow woman; they abandoned the robbery of one bank because one of the Gang found that the president was a former boyhood playmate and they just couldn't do that to him; John had disarmed a colored man that Sheriff Baker had sent into a camp to kill John, and when the man started begging him not to shoot, John had given him a five-dollar bill and had told him to get running.

John Ashley and his large family of brothers and sisters were known to be polite to their elders and thoughtful of persons in need. One of his neighbors stated that he was "real good-hearted — would give you the shirt off his back if you needed it."

Mrs. Nels Jorgensen, one of the Scandinavian pioneers who settled in White City, a settlement near Fort Pierce, Florida, told this story about a member of the Ashley family.

Mrs. Jorgensen, a young nurse, had an urgent request from a neighbor to go to his wife who was in child-birth labor, while he went into Fort Pierce for the doctor. There were no telephones in White City, few cars anyplace, and a two-hour ride by horse and wagon to fetch the doctor.

As Mrs. Jorgensen walked through the woods, she was stopped by a rope stretched across the trail and a masked gunman. He told her to turn back, or she would be shot. She could see men unloading liquor down the way. She could think only of that young mother who needed her. She shook her finger at the gunman and said, "I'm on my way to help a young mother who is having a baby. I'll not be stopped. And don't you stop her husband and the doctor when they come!"

She crawled under the rope, and was allowed on her way. Her husband and the doctor were allowed passage when they came.

There were no four-wheel drive vehicles in the days of prohibition. The Ashleys had to use rented mules and wagons to haul the heavy loads of whiskey from their stills to the paved roads. There the contraband would be loaded into cars for delivery.

Ashley showed great concern for the livery stable owner. He devised a plan that would prevent the owner from being implicated in these illegal activities. He had the owner write out an undated bill of sale to keep to show the authorities if the Ashleys should be caught while using the mules and wagons on a haul. Each time they used the wagons, they would give the owner the purchase price, and he reimbursed the amount above the rental price when they were safely returned to the livery stable.

All of these stories began to represent John as a modern Robin Hood; but, for those who had suffered at his hands, he was a vicious criminal.

Sheriff Baker received John's bullet and message from

the taxi driver, and he determined, that February day in 1924, to accept the invitation. He rounded up a posse and headed for the location of a still where John and his family were supposed to be camping. They arrived at dawn and opened fire on the camp. Deputy Fred Baker was leading the posse and Deputies Elmer Padgett, H. L. Stubbs, Sim Jackson, Oley Bonar, Grover Pass, Ernest Malpurs, and Joe Padgett were aiding him. Joe Ashley was killed inside the tent as he was putting on his boots. John, seeing his father fall, rushed out and shot Fred Baker, then fled into the swamps with others from his gang.[38]

Many townspeople were outraged at the murder of Fred Baker and the continued escape of the outlaws. A large group collected and burned down the camp; then they went to the Ashley and Mobley homes and burned them to the ground.[39]

The Ashley Gang found, on one of their rum-running trips from the Bahamas, that the load of three gallon jugs for which they had paid a premium price, contained only water. They plotted their revenge. West End and Bimini had been settled by rum distributors and their wholesale warehouses had been constructed there. John called in all available members of the Gang. Something went amiss, however, and they had to change their plans to dodge the lawmen who had been alerted. They finally outwitted the deputies, left through Hobe Sound, entered the

Atlantic by using the Inlet at the Jupiter Narrows, and went to Bimini where they raided four wholesale liquor houses. The owners reported that they had been robbed of approximately $8,000 in money and liquor. The Ashley's luck was beginning to run out, for on the morning of the raid, the Bimini dealers had sent $250,000 by express boat to Nassau. [40]

Sheriff Bob Baker was frantic to stop the crime spree of this band of outlaws. It was nearing election time, and their continued freedom and lawless activities would surely be used against him. Baker told Hix Stuart that he had learned that the Ashleys were planning to go up to Jacksonville to hide out with a sister for awhile, rob a bank up that way, and then return after elections to kill Sheriff Baker in revenge for their father's death and the burning of their homes. Then they planned to leave the state.

Baker decided that he should send word to Sheriff Merritt in Saint Lucie County that the outlaws were going up that way, and ask Merritt to try to capture them at the Sebastian Bridge that was twenty-eight miles above Fort Pierce. Baker said that if he and his deputies started up that way, he was certain that friends of the Ashleys would become suspicious and tip them off. He sent a telegram to Merritt and Merritt agreed to cooperate. Baker sent his deputies, Elmer Padgett, Henry Stubbs, L. B. Thomas, and O. B. Padgett. Merritt took two of his deputies, Wiggins and Smith. They blocked off the bridge with a chain that they borrowed from a Sebastian resident, J. T. Thompson, and hung a red lantern in the center of the chain. The deputies then hid in the bushes along the side of the road to await the outlaws. Sheriff Merritt had left his car parked at the north end of the bridge.[41]

The Ashley Gang took their time going up the coast. They stopped in Fort Pierce and were seen on the street. John strolled past a real estate office and nodded to the owner through the window. He went into a barber shop for a haircut and shave. Later he played a game of pool. Lee Gaban, a teenager, was working that day and recalled seeing him there. It was dark when they left Fort Pierce.[42]

Another car arrived at the bridge just ahead of the Ashleys with two Sebastian youths, Ted Miller and S. O. Davis. Sheriff Merritt came out of the bushes, lowered the chain, and told the boys that he would like for them to drive him to his car across the bridge. He jumped on the running board and they drove him across. When the Ashley Gang arrived at the bridge, they had to stop. Riding in the car were John Ashley, Ray Lynn, Clarence Middleton, and John's young nephew, Hanford Mobley. Immediately the deputies swarmed out of the bushes and up to the car. As Miller and Davis turned around and came back across the bridge, their headlights picked up four men in handcuffs lined up along the road. They rushed back to town to tell folks that the Ashley Gang had been captured and handcuffed on the bridge.[43]

Lester Lewis, a grove worker on the E. Sydney Williams grove, also worked part-time for the W. I. Fee Hardware Store and Mortuary.

Lewis told Mr. Williams that he was at the mortuary when the bodies of the men were brought in the night they were killed. He said that the bodies, still handcuffed, were stacked in the car like cord wood. The bodies were later put on display on the grass, with the handcuffs removed, and the curious gathered to stare at them.

Lewis was not called as a witness at the inquest.

Early the next morning, four bullet-riddled bodies were stretched out on the sidewalk in front of Fee Hardware and Mortuary at the corner of Second Street and Avenue A. Crowds soon gathered to stare at the bodies of the vicious outlaws who had terrorized the area for a decade. Many citizens were elated and relieved.

Judge Angus Sumner impaneled a coroner's jury. The news began to be whispered, then spoken aloud; rumors flew that the men had been handcuffed and murdered in cold blood. At the inquest, the Palm Beach deputies were represented by C. D. Abbott; the Saint Lucie deputies were represented by H. J. Dame. The Ashley women had heard the rumors about the handcuffs. They were deeply grieved, and they engaged a young attorney, Alto L.

Adams who had arrived in Fort Pierce in January of that year, to represent the family.[44]

Mrs. Ashley, John's mother, told a story quite different from that of Sheriff Baker. She said that Hanford Mobley had returned from his jobs out of state and had convinced John and the others that they should leave the state with him and seek employment so that they could live a good life, and not always have to be on the run from the law. She said that John had a large sum of money in a money belt, and that they were "going straight." They planned to send for her and the others when they were permanently located. She insisted that they had been handcuffed and murdered "for no reason whatsoever."

The inquest was held. Attorney Adams made a motion that the bodies be exhumed to examine the wrists. The bodies had been embalmed by W. I. Fee and then released to the families.

After Attorney Adams made his motion, some of the jury seemed interested. The judge then declared that the panel had become material witnesses and could not serve as an impartial jury. He disbanded that jury and impaneled another jury later. They listened to the deputies' testimony and ruled the case justifiable homicide.[45]

The Ashleys took the bodies of John, Hanford Mobley, and Ray Lynn to Gomez to be buried in their private family cemetery. They placed the caskets in the

Mobley store so that friends and family could pay their last respects. Mrs. Ashley wanted a Christian burial, but they were not affiliated with any church. Laura Upthegrove sent a request to the Salvation Army, and they sent some of their group up to conduct the graveside service. The mother wept bitterly, repeating that they had been murdered "for no reason at all." Daily she walked the sandy path from her house to the little graveyard, grieving for her husband, her two sons, and the other two sons who had been lost at sea. All five had met violent deaths.

The deputies testified that the men tried to resist arrest, and that they were reaching for their guns. After the inquest, each took an oath that he would never discuss the matter with anyone. Their testimony before the coroner's jury would be their last and only statement.

Those men on the bridge that night kept that oath. Rumor swirled around and public sentiment began to change. The officers that were ridiculed for so long for not being able to arrest and stop the band of robber-killers, suddenly were suspects. Many citizen began to fear an officer's decision to be judge, jury, and executioner.

The capture and slaying occurred November 1, 1924. Three days later, Sheriff Merritt was elected Sheriff of Saint Lucie County, an office that he had held for two years by appointment by Governor Cary Hardee. At first he was the hero of the day, but as time passed, and he proved to be a strict enforcer of the law and unusually adept at catching rum-runners, his popularity began to wane with certain citizens. As his next election neared, the ugly rumors were voiced again and again, and he was defeated as High Sheriff of Saint Lucie County.[46]

With the passing of time, the lawlessness of the Ashleys, who were no longer on the scene, receded in most citizens' memories. The controversial subject of the deputies' conduct on the bridge, however, persisted. They were still around to remind people of unanswered questions. The subject was freshly argued each election year as J. R. Merritt was elected county commissioner, and was reelected term after term. His opponents always revived the subject and suspicion as a possible issue to help defeat him. Through the years, at election time, his children and grandchildren would be taunted about it; his family would be hurt by the campaign mud slinging. So it was for the other deputies and their families.[47]

The Ashley and Mobley families suffered the taunts also. Harassment came from other sources as newsmen and writers would seek interviews as they began to attempt to glamorize Florida's very own gang of outlaws. Each reporter or writer seemed oblivious of the wounds that were reopened, or the taunts from school children who learned for the first time that certain of their classmates were children of former outlaws.[48]

Periodically both of these groups were forced to be publicized, and each time these innocent ones suffered.

Several months ago, the last of the deputies died. Now the final chapter can be written, and perhaps a story that once aroused so much passion can be viewed in an objective but still a humane fashion.

One deputy, before his death, confided to this researcher his memory of the events on the Sebastian Bridge, and he requested that the story not be told as long as any of the deputies lived. That confidence was honored, and for reasons of compassion, his name shall not be revealed. This is the story he told:

The Ashleys were apprehended, as described by others. The deputies knew that they had a group of desperados who had a history of cold-blooded murder, trickery, and a record of escaping every posse and every jail to which they had been confined. They were determined that the Gang would not be given a chance to escape this time. Sheriff Merritt had gone back to his car at the north end of the bridge just as the Ashley Gang drove up. The deputies surrounded them, ordered them out of the car and out on the side of the road. John Ashley was separated from the others, and quickly handcuffed. He was told to hold his hands high above his head and not to move a fraction or he would be shot. The deputy guarding Ashley was "on guard," for Ashley was daring, full of tricks, and could have a sleeve gun concealed that had been overlooked in the first rush to apprehend him. The other deputies were hastily getting the handcuffs on the others. Suddenly John Ashley took a quick step forward and started to drop his handcuffed hands, and the deputy guarding him fired. He said that he supposed the other prisoners tried to break, or that the deputies feared that John had fired on him, for suddenly there was a lot of shouting, and all were killed. He did not credit Sheriff Merritt with any of the shooting. He also did not apologize for his act. He made good a threat to John Ashley, and said that John had promised to kill all of them if he had a chance. "It was them or us, at that point," he said.

The deputy said that he stooped down and scooped out John Ashley's glass eye so that Bob Baker could keep his promise to John to wear it as a watch fob. "But do you know," he said, "they made us send it back so that it could be buried with his body? If I'd known that, I'd have smashed it under my heel on the bridge that night."[49] The bullet and the glass eye truly symbolized the deep hatred shared by these outlaws and these lawmen.

Sheriff Merritt supported his deputies. They had been

given an assignment that he felt was Sheriff Baker's responsibility. He once remarked to a grandson that Baker was afraid of the Ashleys and they knew it. That was the reason they had been able to prey upon the area for so long. Sheriff Merritt was a product of his times. A High Sheriff of a county was intrusted with the security of the citizens, and was the local law. He had been given the charge to stop the Ashleys in his county and he did it — no matter in what manner it had to be done. As far as he was concerned, the cause of justice had been served, and the area would no longer be terrorized by the Ashley Gang.

In 1983, for the first time, the Merritt family agreed to open Sheriff Merritt's files for the purpose of this research. Because he was a man of action and not of words, he never attempted to answer his accusers, nor did he defend his actions with the words of his supporters. This report will do it for him. His files were filled with letters of praise and appreciation from the Honorable John Martin (a governor of Florida for whom Martin County was named when it was created in 1925), law firms all over the state, the Ministerial Association, the United States Postal Inspector, the United States Internal Revenue Service, City and County officials all over the State, doctors, merchants, bank presidents, and countless numbers of citizens. His critics had gone public, while he had kept the letters of his many supporters private. He and the others kept their vow of silence after the ruling of the coroner's inquest.

J. R. Merritt's grandsons said that their grandfather seldom talked of his days as sheriff. Once he told them, however, that he would have been a very wealthy man if he had accepted the bribes offered from the rum-runners.[50]

John Ashley once said that there was one sheriff he hoped he never met face to face, and that was Merritt; he said that he would meet his equal, and one of them would be dead.

The family of DeSoto Tiger heard of John Ashley's death, and they felt that only now had their loved one's death been avenged.[51]

The Ashley and Mobley children decided that their only release from the harassment of writers, reporters, and movie makers was to change their names — and many of them did. Today, only one member of those two immediate families retains the name. He also agreed to an interview for this story but asked that his anonymity be respected. Since he is deceased, he can now be identified. He was Bill Mobley, younger brother of Hanford. His final words, at the end of the interview were: "Why reopen the wounds? None of the children could bear to carry the pain of the name; now they have different names. None of the bodies could rest in their graves; vandals and ghouls desecrated each one — there's not a bone in any of them."

The stories about the activities of the Ashley Gang are numerous, so only a representative few have been used with those documented activities that were dealt with in the courts.

This information has been added to these recorded incidents, information withheld for over half a century: the true relationship of John Ashley and DeSoto Tiger, the true story of the capture on the Sebastian Bridge, and the feelings expressed by the last living member of the Ashley-Mobley families.

Laura Upthegrove later moved to Okeechobee, then to Canal Point, where she continued to bootleg liquor from a small store. There, during an argument over change from a sale of liquor, in a fit of temper, she jerked a bottle of Lysol from a shelf, drank from it, and died. One of Laura's relatives, in an interview with Fran Kerce for *The News Tribune*, October 23, 1977, said that Laura had tried to persuade Mrs. Ashley to stop John from making the trip up the coast that day. Deputy Elmer Padgett told this researcher, in an interview in the 1950's, that Laura had flagged him down and had told him about the planned trip. He felt that she was outraged that John was leaving Florida and not taking her. He, of course, had gone straight to Sheriff Baker with the news.

Laura Upthegrove's younger brother, the late Dewitt Upthegrove, served as Supervisor of Elections in Palm

Beach County for sixteen years, and represented the Democrats of that county as State Committeeman for many years. One of his daughters said that the family was so embarrassed about Laura's notoriety that he was determined to be a good, contributing citizen.

The setting and citizenry described in the beginning of this story was intended to explain the atmosphere of the area and the attitudes of those who lived there during the Ashley Gang era.

While the "Bad Boys" lived by their own laws, often the "Good Boys" did the same, evinced by the mob burning of the Ashley and Mobley homes, and by the manner of the Coroner's Jury's investigation. These events vividly dramatize the frontier conditions that still prevailed on the lower east coast of Florida when the rest of America was entering the modern twentieth century.

(Courtesy: Positive Images)

SHERIFF R. C. ("BOB") BAKER, UNDER WHOSE LEADERSHIP THE ASHLEY GANG WAS EXTERMINATED.

(Courtesy: Positive Images)

JOHN ASHLEY AND HIS SWEETHEART, LAURA UPTHEGROVE.

(Courtesy: Positive Images)

REENACTMENT OF SECOND ROBBERY OF STUART BANK.
HANFORD MOBLEY DISGUISED AS WOMAN.

(Courtesy: Positive Images)

CORRESPONDENCE AND ARTICLES COLLECTED BY THE AUTHOR

JOHN W. MARTIN
JACKSONVILLE, FLORIDA

Nov. 4, 1924.

Hon. J. R. Merritt,
   Ft. Pierce, Fla.

Dear Sheriff:-

   Please accept my congratulations on the splendid work that you and your deputies have done for Florida.

   With kindest regards, I am,

                    Yours sincerely,

JWM:MM
                    John W. Martin

John W. Martin
Jacksonville, Florida

Nov. 4, 1924.

Hon. J. R. Merritt,
Ft. Pierce, Fla.

Dear Sheriff:-

Please accept my congratulations on the splendid work that you and your deputies have done for Florida.

With kindest regards, I am,

Yours sincerely,
John W. Martin

TREASURY DEPARTMENT

BUREAU OF INTERNAL REVENUE

WASHINGTON

OFFICE OF
FEDERAL PROHIBITION COMMISSIONER

January 3, 1925.

Hon. I. R. Meritt, Sheriff,
   Ft. Pierce,
      St. Lucie County, Fla.

Dear Sir:

    Letters recently received from Mr. A. L. Allen, Federal Prohibition Director for the State of Florida, and Mr. H. L. Duncan, Divisional Chief, General Prohibition Agents, contain a statement to the effect that you have done as much as anyone in the State of Florida in connection with the enforcement of Prohibition; that you have not only driven each and every bootlegger out of your county, but also go outside of your county in order to assist in enforcement of the Prohibition laws.

    I am glad to receive such information in order that I may thank you and join the Director and Divisional Chief in an expression of appreciation of your very successful work.

                              Yours very truly,

                              R. A. HAYNES
                         Prohibition Commissioner.

Treasury Department
Bureau of Internal Revenue
Washington
January 3, 1925.

Hon. I. R. Merritt, Sheriff,
Ft. Pierce,
St. Lucie County, Fla.

Dear Sir:

Letters recently received from Mr. A. L. Allen, Federal Prohibition Director for the State of Florida, and Mr. H. L. Duncan, Divisional Chief, General Prohibition Agents, contain a statement to the effect that you have done as much as anyone in the State of Florida in connection with the enforcement of Prohibition; that you have not only driven each and every bootlegger out of your county, but also go outside of your county in order to assist in enforcement of the Prohibition laws.

I am glad to receive such information in order that I may thank you and join the Director and Divisional Chief in an expression of appreciation of your very successful work.

Yours very truly,
R. A. Hayes
Prohibition Commissioner.

THE MINISTERIAL ASSOCIATION OF FORT PIERCE, FLORIDA

We desire to commend most heartily, the proposed action of our sheriff J.R.Merritt, with regard to the inforcement of the Sunday laws of this State, as set forth in the published account in the Fort Pierce papers.
We believe that the preservation of the rest day, commonly known as Sunday, is vital to the truest welfare of a community.
At this time the establishment and inforcement of law, is of the greatest importance.
Therefore we desire to express our highest appreciation of all that our sheriff J.R.Merritt, has done, for the establishing the supremecy of law in Saint Lucie County, and we assure him of our heartiest support in carring out the laws of our State and the Nation.
And we therefore urge the lawabiding people of the county to support him with their sympathy and co operation.

    Done by order the Ministerial association on conferance, this 10th. day of March 1926, and ordered signed by the president and secretary of this association.

    Signed _J. M. Lewis,_ president

    Signed _H. M. Barnett,_ Secretary

THE MINISTERIAL ASSOCIATION OF FORT PIERCE, FLORIDA

We desire to commend most heartily, the proposed action of our sheriff J. R. Merritt, with regard to the enforcement of the Sunday laws of this State, as set forth in the published account in the Fort Pierce papers. We believe that the preservation of the rest day, commonly known as Sunday is vital to the truest welfare of a community.

At this time the establishment and enforcement of law is of the greatest importance.

Therefore we desire to express our highest appreciation of all that our sheriff J. R. Merritt has done, for the establishing the supremacy of law in Saint Lucie County, and we assure him of our heartiest support in carrying out the laws of our State and the Nation.

And we therefore urge the law abiding people of the county to support him with their sympathy and co operation.

Done by order the Ministerial association on conference, this 10th day of March 1926, and ordered signed by the president and secretary of this association.

Signed J. M. Lewis, President
Signed H. M. Barnett, Secretary

FORT PIERCE BANK AND TRUST CO.

STATE, COUNTY AND CITY DEPOSITORY

E. L. PRICE
PRESIDENT

FORT PIERCE, FLORIDA

Nov. 21, 1924.

Mr. J. R. Merritt,
City.

Dear Mr. Merritt:-

    Yesterday at our Director's meeting, we mentioned the valiant services rendered by you and your deputies some weeks ago in handling the Ashley Gang. The Board of Directors passed a resolution authorizing us to write you a letter endorsing the splendid work and expressing to you our appreciation for the accomplishment. As a further expression of our appreciation, the Directors of this institution authorized us to enclose check for the use of yourself and deputies for $300.00.

    We hope you will accept this and the spirit in which it is intended and that you may find some satisfaction and encouragement by the action of our Board.

    I am also enclosing a check for $25.00 from the Peoples Bank of Okeechobee as an expression of their good wishes and appreciation for your efforts in this same undertaking.

Yours very truly,

President

ELP/c

Enclosures.

Fort Pierce Bank and Trust Co.
State, County and City Depository
Fort Pierce, Florida
Nov. 21, 1924

Mr. J. R. Merritt
City.

Dear Mr. Merritt:-

 Yesterday at our Director's meeting, we mentioned the valiant services rendered by you and your deputies some weeks ago in handling the Ashley Gang. The Board of Directors passed a resolution authorizing us to write you a letter endorsing the splendid work and expressing to you our appreciation for the accomplishment. As a further expression of our appreciation, the Directors of this institution authorized us to enclose check for the use of yourself and deputies for $300.00.
 We hope you will accept this and the spirit in which it is intended and that you may find some satisfaction and encouragement by the action of our Board.
 I am also enclosing a check for $25.00 from the Peoples Bank of Okeechobee as an expression of their good wishes and appreciation for your efforts in this same undertaking.

      Yours very truly,
      E. L. Price
      President

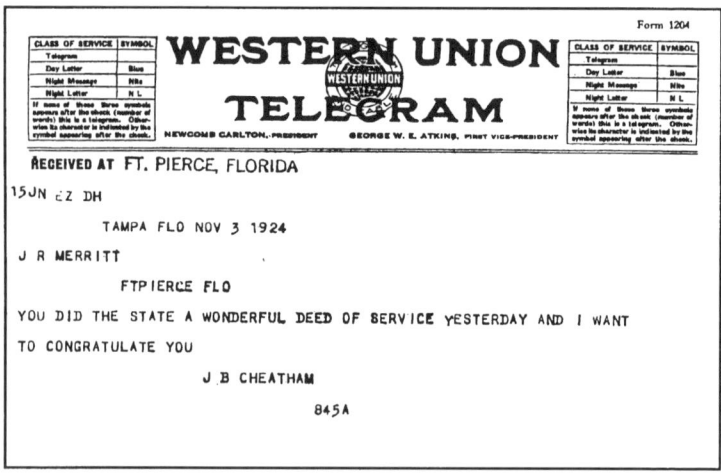

Received at Ft. Pierce, Florida
Tampa, Flo Nov. 3, 1924

J. R. Merritt
Ft. Pierce, Flo
You did the State a wonderful deed of service yesterday and I want to congratulate you
    J. B. Cheatham
    8:45 A

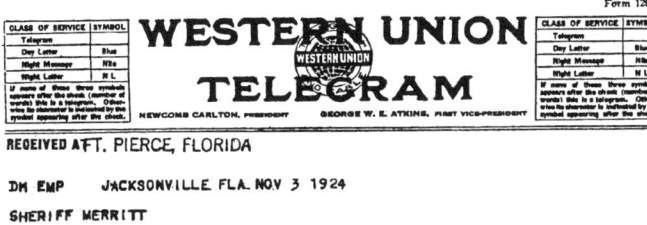

Received at Ft. Pierce, Florida
Jacksonville, Fla. Nov. 3 1924

Sheriff Merritt
Ft. Pierce, Fla.
Good boy. After my good friend Bingham of Palm Beach serves the coming term it's Merritt next.
      Merrick

GEO. W. HOLMES. M.D.
Local Surgeon F. E. C. Railway

SHARPES, FLORIDA, 11 6 1924

Sheriff Merrett & Deputies
Gentlemen
Your efficient conduct in putting an end to the Ashley Gang at the Sebastian Bridge deserves the approval of all Law Abiding Men —

The possession of fire arms is good, full of intended use of them by our Bootlegging Scoundrels "Shoot to Kill" is the word "Do unto others as they do to you and do it first" is a safe Motto. Formed good, but weak men are seduced from the paths of rectitude, as they note the ease with which criminals escape with the aid of their accomplice called Lawyers.

With Sentiments of the highest esteem for each one of you I am your admirer

Geo W Holmes

Geo. W. Holmes, M.D.
Local Surgeon, F. E. C. Railway

                      Sharpes, Florida, 11-6-1924

Sheriff Merritt & Deputies
Gentlemen,

  Your efficient conduct in putting an end to the Ashley Gang at the Sebastian Bridge deserves the approval of all law abiding men.

  The possession of fire arms is good proof of intended use of them by our bootlegging scoundrel. Shoot to kill is the word. "Do unto others as they do to you and do it first" is a safe motto.

  Former good, but weak, men are seduced from the paths of rectitude as they note the ease with which criminals escape with the aid of their accomplices <u>called Lawyers</u>.

  With sentiments of the highest esteem for each one of you, I am your admirer

                      George W. Holmes

Post Office Department

OFFICE C.F INSPECTOR   CASE No.

Inspector

New York N.y. Nov 3, 1924

Subject:

Mr J R Merritt, Sheriff
  Fort Pierce Fla

Dear Sheriff,

    I wish to congratulate you on the great result obtained in the extinction of the Ashley gang by you and your officers.

    You have performed a great public service and I trust it will be fully appreciated by the public.

Very truly yours,
Herbert N Graham

Post Office Department
Office of Inspector
New York, NY Nov. 3, 1924

Mr. J. R. Merritt, Sheriff
Fort Pierce, Fla.

Dear Sheriff,

I wish to congratulate you on the great result obtained in the extinction of the Ashley gang by you and your officers.

You have performed a great public service and I trust it will be fully appreciated by the public.

Very truly yours,
Herbert N. Graham

FIRST BAPTIST CHURCH
COR. BREVARD AVE. AND OAK ST.

REV. OLLIE L. RIGGS, PASTOR
COCOA, FLORIDA

Nov. 4, 1924.

Mr. J. R. Merritt,
Fort Pierce, Fla.

Dear Sir:

Please accept my congratulations for your efforts and success in cleaning up the Ashley band. You have won the confidence of the best people of this section. I hope we may have more men of your type to inforce our laws.

With many good wishes,

I am

Very respectfully yours,

O. L. Riggs

First Baptist Church
Cor. Brevard Ave. And Oak St.
Rev. Ollie L. Riggs, Pastor
Cocoa, Florida

Nov. 4, 1924

Mr. J. R. Merritt
Fort Pierce, Fla.

Dear Sir:

Please accept my congratulations for your efforts and success in cleaning up the Ashley band. You have won the confidence of the best people of this section. I hope we may have more men of your type to enforce our laws.

With many good wishes
I am
Very respectfully yours,
O. L. Riggs

```
                    WM. F. C. FELLERS
                         ADJUSTER
                  No. 2 Main Street   P. O. Box 949
                         Phone 41
                  JACKSONVILLE, FLORIDA      Nov 5th 1924.
```

Mr. P. C. Eldred,
    Fort Pierce, Fla.

Dear Mr Eldred:

    May I have your good offices to convey to Sherriff Merritt my hearty thanks and congratulations on his brilliant work in ridding the people and of StLucie county and the state of Florida of one of its greatest menaces.

    I am sure that I am only one of many hundred that entertain a sense of gratitude to Sheriff Merritt that such a remarkable work was accomplished without the loss of a single life of his staff.

                          Yours truly,

                            Wm F C Fellers

Wm. F. C. Fellers
Adjuster
No. 5 Main Street   P. O. Box 969
Phone 41
Jacksonville, Florida   Nov 5th 1924.

Mr. P. C. Eldred,
Fort Pierce, Fla.

Dear Mr. Eldred:

May I have your good offices to convey to Sheriff Merritt my hearty thanks and congratulations on his brilliant work in ridding the people of St. Lucie county and the state of Florida of one of its greatest menaces.

I am sure that I am only one of many hundred that entertain a sense of gratitude to Sheriff Merritt that such a remarkable work was accomplished without the loss of a single life of his staff.

Yours truly,
William F. C. Fellers

Inquest Into Ashley Gang Killings

FT. PIERCE, NOVEMBER 6, 1924—An inquest into the killing of John Ashley, notorious east coast bandit, and three companions by Sheriff J. R. Merritt and a force of St. Lucie and Palm Beach County deputies at the Sebastian River Bridge last Saturday night came to a sudden halt Wednesday afternoon

The unexpected adjournment of the inquest came after four hours of startling testimony by T. R. Miller and S. 0. Davis, two Sebastian young men, whose evidence tended to show that the four desperadoes might have been shot down while handcuffed and defenseless. No opportunity was afforded the officers to combat this testimony. Another coroner's jury will be empaneled to begin a new inquest at 10 o'clock next Saturday morning.

Sheriff Merritt and the officers who were with him have all been subpoenaed and will tell the jury their versions of the capture of the outlaws, who, they say, were shot down when they made a sudden attempt to draw their guns, after being arrested.

Among the spectators was Mrs. J. W. Ashley, aged mother of the dead bandit leader, surrounded by a small party of friends.

Interest was heightened by the presence of attorneys C. D. Abbott and E. C. Thompson of West Palm Beach, and J. H. Dame of Ft. Pierce, who announced that they were on hand to protect the interests of the officers who took part in the capture. In the jury box were Albert Schuman, S. A. Braswell, George Badger, D. J. Rea, S. H. Bray and L. 0. Baughtman, all of Sebastian, who had been summoned by Sheriff Merritt to serve on the jury immediately after the shooting Saturday night.

That the hearing was about to take an interesting and unusual turn became apparent with the calling of the first witness, W. I. Fee, Ft. Pierce undertaker, who prepared the bodies of the dead bandits for burial. One of the first questions put to him was whether he noticed any marks on the arms of the dead men that might have been caused by handcuffs. He replied that no marks of any kind were evident on their arms.

From the time Mr. Fee was excused until the hearing ended at 3 o'clock, Miller and Davis were on the witness stand, most of the time undergoing a grueling cross examination by Attorney Abbott. In a number of details their stories differed, but their testimony that they saw handcuffs on the a four captives before they were killed was never shaken.

Miller was the first to testify. He said he drove his car up to the Sebastian Bridge about 10:45 o'clock, accompanied by Davis. He was taking Davis home, he testified, and they had decided to go for a drive beforehand.

As they stopped at the barrier that had been placed across the end of the bridge, another car drove up behind them and stopped, Miller said. From the front seat of his car he could see men with guns surrounding the other car and hear the occupants ordered to stick up their hands. He said he saw one of the men on the ground strike a man in the car in the face with his gun.

Thinking a holdup was taking place, Miller said he and his companion began secreting their watches in the top of the car and placing their money under the seat. He then left the car and started to walk out on the bridge, but Davis called to him to come back. Soon after he returned to his car, Miller said, Sheriff Merritt came up and, saying they were capturing the Ashley gang, requested that Miller carry him to his car at the other end of the bridge. On the way over, Miller testified, the sheriff showed him a pearl-handled revolver and told him it was the one he had taken from Ashley.

Miller said that when he and Davis started across the bridge with the sheriff, the four prisoners were standing in the road with their hands in the air, surrounded by officers with their guns trained on them. After a few minutes they returned and leaving their car walked toward their party, he said. He testified that he then saw three of the men handcuffed together, and John Ashley standing to one side with a pair of handcuffs on his wrists.

"These boys are going to Sebastian and want to get by," Sheriff Merritt told the other officers, so Miller testified, and he and Davis entered their car and drove toward town. They passed the prisoners slowly and plainly saw the handcuffs on their arms, he declared. Arriving in town they met several men, including Mr. Schuman, Mr. Braswell and Mr. Badger and told them the Ashley gang had been captured and the officers had them handcuffed back at the bridge, Miller stated. In the meantime, he said, Sheriff Merritt had driven into Sebastian by another road and went to the depot, where he reported the shooting of the prisoners.

Miller testified that he returned to the scene of the capture with several members of the coroner's jury and looked at the bodies. On the arms of two of them, he said, he saw marks that he supposed were caused by the handcuffs.

This was the essence of the story related by Miller, and a long cross examination by Mr. Abbott and members of the jury failed to change it in any essential particular.

FT. PIERCE - NOVEMBER 8, 1924—Justifiable homicide was the unanimous verdict of the second coroner's jury empaneled Saturday to investigate the killing of John Ashley, bandit leader, and three companions by St. Lucie and Palm Beach County officers at the Sebastian Bridge on the night of November 1.

Sheriff Merritt and the deputies who assisted in the capture of the Ashley gang all took the stand and refuted the testimony given by previous hearing to the effect at they saw Ashley and his companions handcuffed before they were shot.

James R. (J.R.) Merritt, Sheriff, St. Lucie County, Florida
(Courtesy: St. Lucie County Historical Museum)

Flatwoods Scene, Artist, Bill Mobley, brother of Hanford and nephew of John Ashley

John Ashley wearing eye patch, with unnamed bystander
(Courtesy: Fort Lauderdale Historical Society)

McCASKILL, TAYLOR & McCASKILL
LAWYERS
RALSTON BUILDING
MIAMI, FLORIDA

O. E. McCASKILL
H. H. TAYLOR
J. M. McCASKILL

November 3, 1924.

Sheriff J. R. Merrit,
Fort Pierce, Fla.

Dear Sir:-

     Please accept my hearty congratulations to you and your force for your complete annihilation of the Ashley gang.

     You will not receive congratulations in writing or in person from the large number of people who are congratulating you to various persons to whom they talked. It was a clever piece of work on the part of you and your force. Whatever the circumstances were surrounding the annihilation, everybody says, is immaterial so long as you caught them and killed them, but people generally are thankful to you for your stategy and the work you did when you caught them.

     Very sincerely yours,

     [signature]

McCaskill, Taylor & McCaskill
Lawyers
Ralston Building
Miami, Florida

G. E. McCaskill
H. H. Taylor
J. M. McCaskill

November 3, 1924

Sheriff J. R. Merritt
Fort Pierce, Fla.

Dear Sir:-

Please accept my hearty congratulations to you and your force for your complete annihilation of the Ashley gang.

You will not receive congratulations in writing or in person from the large number of people who are congratulating you to various persons to whom they talk. It was a clever piece of work on the part of you and your force. Whatever the circumstances were surrounding the annihilation, everybody says, is immaterial so long as you caught them and killed them, but people generally are thankful to you for your strategy and the work you did when you caught them.

Very sincerely yours,
G. E. McCaskill

NOTES

1. Hix C. Stuart, *The Notorious Ashley Gang* (Stuart, Florida: St. Lucie Printing Co., Inc., 1928), pp. 7-8.

2. Alfred J. Hanna and Kathryn A. Hanna, *Lake Okeechobee* (New York: The Bobbs-Merrill Co., 1948), pp. 204 -205.

3. Stuart, p.8.

4. Personal interview with Frank Shore, Seminole Indian Reservation, 20 March 1983.

5. Hanna, p. 205.

6. Frank Shore, interview with a Seminole chief and medicine man

7. Stuart, p. 9.

8. Ibid., pp. 10-11.

9. *The Stuart Times* (alternating as the *Stuart Messenger* at times) located in Stuart, Florida. All of the notes attributed to this source are more fully documented in the text of the paper.

10. Stuart, pp. 11-12.

11. Ibid. , p. 12.

12. *The Stuart Times.*

13. *Ibid.*

14. Personal interview with John Taylor, Stuart, Florida, 1957.

15. Ibid.

16. *The Stuart News,* 50th Anniversary Edition, 9 January 1964.

17. *The Stuart News*, 19 February 1915.

18. *Ibid.*, 3 May 1915.

19. Personal interview with William Lee Coats, Fort Pierce, Florida, 1957.

20. Personal interview with Mrs. Cecia Stuart Green and Mrs. Lottie Lee Deberry, daughters of Hix Stuart, Stuart, Florida, April 1983.

21. *The Stuart Times*, Anniversary Edition.

22. *The Stuart Times.*

23. *Ibid.*

24. Hanna, p. 207.

25. *The Stuart Times*, 6 June 1921.

26. *Ibid.*, 23 July 1915.

27. *The Stuart Times* Anniversary Edition

28. Hanna, p. 208.

29. The *Stuart Messenger.*

30. Stuart, pp. 20-21.

31. Ibid., pp. 25-26.

32. Interview with John E. Taylor.

33. Stuart, p. 32.

34. Ibid., pp. 33-34.

35. Personal interview with Elmer Padgett, Palm City, Florida, 1958.

36. The *Stuart Messenger* and a personal interview with Ed. Merritt, grandson of Sheriff J. R. Merritt, Fort Pierce, Florida, February 1983.

37. Stuart, pp. 36-37.

38. Elmer Padgett interview.

39. Hanna, P. 210, and personal interview with Bill Mobley, brother of Hanford and a member of the Ashley family.

40. Personal interview with anonymous member of the Ashley-Mobley families.

41. *The Stuart News*, Anniversary Edition.

42. Jerry Bowers, "Ashley Gang," *The Miami Herald*, 12 January 1969

43. *Ibid.*

44. Personal interview with the Honorable Alto L. Adams, Retired Judge of the Supreme Court of Florida, at the Adams Ranch Library, Fort Pierce, Florida, February 1983.

45. Ibid.; also, a personal interview with Judge Angus Sumner, Fort Pierce, Florida, 1957.

46. Ed Merritt interview, grandson of Sheriff Merritt.

47. Interview with Ed and Dwyane Merritt, grandsons of J. R. Merritt in Fort Pierce, Florida, 13 April, 1983.

48. Interview with anonymous Ashley family members.

49. Personal interview with anonymous deputy.

50. Ed and Dwyane Merritt interview.

51. Personal interview with Flora Tiger Jones (deceased), daughter of DeSoto Tiger, and Ada Micco Tiger (deceased) wife of DeSoto Tiger, Fort Pierce, Florida, 1957; and personal interview with Louise Jones, granddaughter of D. Tiger, 1983.

Many individual citizens in Martin, Saint Lucie, Okeechobee, and Indian River Counties were interviewed over a period of thirty years. Many have asked that they not be identified. Several members of the

Ashley Gang volunteered information and also asked to remain anonymous.

Special thanks to Angus Sumner for many hours of invaluable assistance.